How She Came Here

How She Came Here

Poems by

Barbara Elovic

Cover Design: Shay Culligan
Cover image by Amy Durocher, *Manhattan Bridge*
Author photo by Martine Bisagni

Library of Congress Control Number: 2022935579

ISBN: 978-1-63980-111-4

Kelsay Books
502 South 1040 East, A-119
American Fork, Utah 84003
Kelsaybooks.com

To my many teachers and friends

Acknowledgments

Alehouse: "The Chagall Dance
Big City Lit: "Alice Paul"
Bridges: "Midrash from Enid"
Connecticut Review: "Union Square"
Erbacce: "Dorothea's Foot"
Exquisite Corpse: "Imelda," "Landlord Hell"
Heliotrope: "Chuck Jones Tribute," "Leap of Faith," "Susan B."
Home Planet News: "Brooklyn Bound"
Lips: "My Father Meets Celebrities While Flying on Business"
The Marlboro Review: "Moonshine"
Movieworks: "Happy Ending"
MSS: "Maybe"
Patterson Literary Review: "Anne Frank"
Philadelphia Inquirer Blog: "Poem Without a Solution"
Piedmont Literary Review: "Isaac's Sacrifice"
Pivot: "Angels," "Parade," "The Sad Magicians," "Time Out"
Poetry: "Afterward," "Light Years," "Schooling"
Onthebus: "The Lineup"
Oxford Magazine: "Snowmen"
The Same: "Curious George"
Saranac Review: "Eve's Version"
Shrew: "Lee Miller," "That Statue," "Zelda"
Word Thursdays: "Unfinished Business"

Anthologies:
I Speak of the Cities: "Brooklyn Bound"
Like Light: "Art, Credo"
Many Lights in Many Windows: "Angels"
To Genesis: "Isaac's Sacrifice," "You Think You Got Problems?"
Walk on the Wild Side: "Brooklyn Bound"
You Are Here: "Brooklyn Bound"

"My Father Meets Celebrities While Flying on Business and "Time Out" also appeared in the chapbook *Time Out*.

Sixteen poems in this book also appeared in the chapbook *Other People's Stories*.

Thanks to Patricia Aakre, Carl Rosenstock, and Michael T. Young who saw these poems in earlier versions and helped make them better.

Contents

Part I

Maybe

Not the alarm clock but
hope gets you out of bed in the morning,
lets you sit at your parents' table
where you may not secure their blessing
but at least may eat it peace.

It's hope that makes you run away from home
believing that starting over in another place
can make a difference, lets you ask
directions of the stranger on the street
not knowing if he'll mislead you

once he knows you're lost.
You place one foot in front of the other
holding on to nothing
even when the ground gives way.
Hope is the goat cart you ride in crippled.

Secretly you make a wish
under a sky crazy with stars
hoping that the light you've chosen
doesn't come from a source already dead.

Schooling

Before we go anywhere
we line up by size.

Others lean over their desks
waving both hands. I wait,
my arm held taut as her yardstick.
Call on me.
My ears burn when I give the wrong answer.

Miss Brown reviews us row by row
to check for germs.
I must drop my hands into hers.
She turns one over, then the other.

When Jimmy Cole calls
Miss Brown, "Mommy,"
we laugh.

Each time she is absent
we hope she is dead.

Later when others cut school
with excuses they write themselves
I can be found
in the fifth seat from the front.
Where the alphabet is law
I know my place.

Light Years

Didn't I have the name picked out
for my eventual stardom?
I practiced signing autographs

at seven. I knew I'd rise
above the dust motes when my mother
handed me the chamois and the Pledge.

I wouldn't have time to bother
matching napkins to Melmac plates,
even if there's something strangely

pretty in golden fleurs-de-lys
repeating over embossed tissue
paper, devised just to throw away.

What difference whether I folded
them so that their ends met?
Their pattern more regular

and predictable than the stars,
the stars far away and cold
as I longed to be.

My Father Meets Celebrities While
Flying on Business

Twenty years before there are computers
in every American family room
my father shuttles across the country
and beyond buying and selling chips
and talking semiconductors.
I'm seven years old
and not sure what any of this means.
I only know that sometimes my father
is away for a month at a time.
He comes home to report that Zsa Zsa's accent
is even funnier than Grandma's
or to tell about the day he sat in first class
next to Paul Newman. Paul's son met him at the airport.
He looked like a slob who needed a shave.
Another time he rode beside a gray-haired man
with a clipped mustache who a friend
across the aisle called Walt.
My father first assumes he's the maker
of Mickey Mouse. But when the man in the dull brown suit sighs,
"Back to the news tomorrow night,"
my father realizes
it's not the cartoonist and lord and master of the Magic Kingdom
to his right, but the darling of TV journalism,
Walter Cronkite. The most trusted man in America
and my dad who shine in their own worlds
hurtle across the sky toward home
where my father gives me
a 14-karat-gold Tinkerbell charm
with her own pair of tiny wings.

How He Left Me

Last night a wounded bird
flew in our window
and lit on my husband's hand.
He's always had a soft spot
for the weak.
Its chest heaved as it flapped
its injured wing.
Then he walked out the front door,
the bird twittering
above his shoulder.
I watched from the window
as he walked farther away.
The bird began to change
under my husband's gaze.
First it perched on the hand
he held aloft,
grew long reedy legs
and for a moment
became a stork.
They kept moving
and soon the bird was a woman
a head taller than he,
as high as his hand had been held.
Their backs to me,
they walked down the street
arm in arm.

Excuse Me

You look like someone
I used to know used to look.
I don't know what he looks like now.
I don't know where he lives
or how he fared.
Has his hair turned gray?
Does he still have hair?
I don't know why I care.
We didn't part friends.
If he died would I hear?
What's he up to now?
Is he rich? Is he well?
Forgive me if I stared.
You look like someone
I used to know used to look.
God knows what he looks like now
or why I should care.

Play Ball

for my ex

This man who'd make a pass at any friend
of mine who might cooperate—
and if not her then her sister—
this man I married took my love
of baseball to a whole new level.

He's the one who taught me how to score a game
how to mark the corners in a box
to denote which base the hitter reached,
the number I should circle to say
which fielder had made the play
to draw an upside-down, inverted K
when a batter was gone on a called strike,
and what to look for in a pitch.

Even though most of his talk was worth
less than the oxygen expended
and outside the ballpark I could never tell
when he was lying,
all these years later
I still love the game.

Unfinished Business

By the time my mother got cancer
my father was twelve years into the disease
that would kill him.
He walked awkwardly,
the different parts of his body
seemingly undecided on which way
to head. So they tried
going different places in the room at once.

My mother had been operated on that morning,
the exploratory procedure from which the surgeon
emerged to tell my father and me
that the mass was too large to cut out,
neglecting to say there were other cures.
Dr. Hot Stuff was done.
so what if his gruff dismissal
led us to believe my mother was done for?

We drove back to the house,
sat in the kitchen.
My father refused my offer of coffee
and then he rose.
His hands curled in loose fists,
he pushed one shoulder forward,
then the opposite leg, over and over.
He was moving

away from the table where I sat stunned.
And not as soon as he'd have liked
he was in the next room
crying

where he thought I couldn't see him.
And I who'd believed
all the family troubles
might be solved

had my father and mother only split up
glimpsed, as my father shuddered
in the laundry room,
one of those unexplained cavities
in the heart where love
and its lack, need and hunger,
lurk unheeded an entire life.

The Lineup

I wait in a bare, blue room
where the walls don't meet
the ceiling. After an hour
of radio static and muffled
sports scores the detective
asks me to identify the perpetrator
by number and to speak up
when I state his crime.
He raps on the wall:
Six men seated at a long table
come into view. Among them
the gap-toothed man with the sloppy mustache.
"That's him." But the table grows
as more people sit behind it:
My mother, number seven, prized me
as her favorite symptom.
There's my brother complaining
I don't show enough interest in his life.
The ninth's my ex-husband whose longing
for distant places took him
to a new woman in another part of the city.
My father grips card number ten before
it falls from his hands. The last time
I saw him he told me he couldn't wait to die.
I must call out their numbers and inform on them.
A gray-shirted sergeant is taking notes.
I'll finger them all but still
be left here standing beside the one-way mirror
where no one can see me.

The Chagall Dance

Lovers and goats orbit a town
that lives only in the sky on a canvas.
I visit Ukraine to see for myself
the world my grandparents fled.
Streton snarls around its one paved road.
The wooden slat houses
have never been painted.
Indoor plumbing and the twenty-first century
have yet to arrive.
But the Jews grew impatient
and flew off to America or the ovens.
A woman in babushka and apron
who looks at least eighty insists
she remembers my family.
Henka Heller was her best friend.
"Who would I ask?" my mother answers
when I wonder if this might be true.
Henka the phantom cousin joins the dance
of creatures conjured from memory or guilt
whose feet never touch the ground.

Snowmen

They stand on the lawns
where they've been left
by the families
who molded them to stand guard
or stare at the sky and wonder

if they've any tie to the stars.
They mistake the column of powdery
light that falls over them
from the living room
for a searchlight.

It draws them
like some promise of grace,
and slowly they pull themselves
to the front door, pausing
longingly by a window

to see the family arranged
around the set, in what looks
like an act of devotion.
Since they haven't been given hands
they bang their heads against the doors

wanting in, losing a little
of themselves in the effort,
not knowing or caring
that the heat inside
will surely do them in.

Midrash from Enid

for Enid Dame, 1943–2003

She enjoyed a jumble of joke
and prayer to make her point.
Puns, which are easy, don't count.
Two parts whistling past the junkyard
with a shmear of laugh or die on the side,
hold the lies.

Where I'm from they'd fold in a tier
of Old Testament ladies, as if
Sarah, Leah, Miriam
were no more than the women's auxiliary
instead of the mothers of a nation—
a clucking chapter of Hadassah
crocheting and cooking,
separate but happy.

Walk this way, I was told. Up the winding
stairs to the Old Country
where unschooled girls in tall tales jumped
down wells when they started their periods
for fear they were bleeding to death
or were married off to men they never met—
all those women
not rating a commentary
or a second opinion.

Enid started elsewhere,
from the kind of family I wished would adopt me
by the time I turned sixteen.
Her people struck for a living wage
or stood vigil for peace.

Nogoodniks, my mother would say.
How ya going to earn a living doing that?
Ya think you're some kind of princess?

In my yeshiva by fifth grade
girls were culled from the boys
to guard the Talmud pages
from our female touch. From twelve on up
we were predictably unclean. No kidding.
I aged and left the rabbis' version behind
seeking room to think and laugh without
being labeled trouble, told not to sulk. Enid lived on

one of those off roads, too, rewriting
the tales they told at my house, taught in my school
to tease and threaten, cajole and bore
so that the stories became both map and legend
toward that oasis or bestiary, *(which is it?)*
where when the lion and the lamb lie down together
they could as easily be a man and a woman.

Time-out

for Lois and Patty

My father has died so we're having brunch.
By my count this is the first time
in eight years we've sat down together for a meal.
Who made our lives too busy
for rest, for time to spend with friends?
I want to talk with the man in charge.
With our luck, he'll turn out to be
some lightweight with a hang-up about his size
who apprenticed as a ref at hockey games.
Too many years of skating on Zambonied ice
after big lugs with sticks and pucks
and he wants more control.

Well, this winter I learned to walk on ice.
Otherwise I wouldn't have gotten to work.
And this winter we buried my dad
in ground too hard to take him in.
After an hour-long fight
with the cemetery staff
who demanded cold cash up front
for access to the family plot.
I stood off to the side,
watching my cousins and the rabbi himself
straining in their suits
and dress shoes, knocking
with their small shovels
on frozen dirt to cover the coffin
of a man who'd been diagnosed
twenty-some years earlier with a disease
that killed him piecemeal.

It's as if that ref decided
his burial should recap
all the power plays by dad endured,
so that at the end
a child's coffin could hold
what was left of him.

I don't talk about the grave
or who presides over it while we eat
bagels and New York-style omelettes,
but I'd like to think it's not too late
to play fair. I want to change the rules

Happy Ending

You never can tell just where or when

Mr. Right will turn up.
Maybe you'll meet him as Natalie Wood did
in *Splendor in the Grass*

in a mental hospital called Shady Rest or Sprawling Green;
anyway a calm place, the kind you have in mind when you sing
    "Blue Skies,"
where no one's craziness is particularly threatening.

The guy's just there because his parents
forced him to become a surgeon, but
he fainted when he had to make his first cut.

Now he's hammering out his rage in metal shop
and hitting on Natalie, he's a sensitive boy really.
Though something of a come down from Warren Beatty,

the boy back home to whom she bids farewell
on the run-down farm of his dreams—he's sweaty, mud-stained,
and married to a woman found on the rebound in New Haven.

Natalie's all white gloves and lace, straw-hatted for spring
which is supposed to hint that a happy ending
wasn't in the cards. Oh well.

The Great Depression is winding down.
She rides away through Kansas consoling
herself with poetry, just like real life.

Landlord Hell

for J. Lazarus, lord of Kings Realty

Though it's over 130 degrees
the pipes rattle and steam hisses from every radiator.
A recorded message repeats twice a minute,
"You've reached the office of Lazarus Realty.
No one is here to take your call. Just pay your rent."
He rues the day he made that tape,
but now the erase button is out of reach.
Benny the super's no help. He's here, too,
but he still can't fix anything.
At least he's stopped drinking
if only because the beer evaporates
as soon as he pops the tab off the can.
Mrs. Goodtimes, lately of 2I,
is now Lazarus' neighbor.
For years she was convinced
that I either taught the fox-trot
or ran a brothel above her
and told anyone so who would listen,
including the police.
She's still screaming at husband Jerry,
though he's safely out of earshot, that she
should never have left Florida for him
to come to such a place. She thinks she's still in Brooklyn.
Lazarus earned the deed to this subterranean tract
by proving himself above. But his current tenants
have paid their way in, so to speak,
so he can't marshal their eviction.
He's stuck with the moaner next door and his memories
and knows he'll never again live up to his name.

It's Not Personal

When you're fired
or worse—an armed guard
escorts you to your cubicle
to clear out your things.
Who knows, you might steal company secrets
or that desk lamp you've loved for years.
Soon you're serving Cheerios for dinner,
or Mac & Cheese on good nights.

And it's not personal that because you're middle-aged
you can't find another job
and start to fall behind on bills.
It's not personal when the lights get turned off, the heat.
Candlelight provides such a homey glow.
Next you're thrown out of your house.
How could that possibly be personal?

When you come right down to it
no one is really a person, just a statistic, a number,
an item in a database. So what the hell!
Go for it. Do what you want—to whomever.
Get a gun. Shoot your ex-boss—the bastard.
We all know,
"It's not personal."

Parade

for Cathleen

Thrown down from office windows,
pages of the old year's calendar sail to the street
Like a flock of birds come to join a celebration.
Days of appointments kept or missed
now mean no more than tickertape.
In our car we've become part of a parade
leaving the business district and last year behind.

I've come west for the holidays,
and for my troubles I'm rewarded
with longer days and bluer skies
and this casual casting off of the old,
which a friend assures me
also happens in Manhattan, though I've never seen it,
lost time tossed aside like so much useless trash.
Endings should always be this happy and this simple.

The Sad Magicians

When magic went bankrupt,
those crafty men in black
had nothing left on account,
let alone up their sleeves.
They found nothing, no small
furry creatures hiding
in their top hats—only
a band of sweat to circle
their heads: no help against
a falling sky. Now that
their scarves refused to fly,
not believing in themselves
enough to become doves,
the magicians packed in
what remained of the tools
of their trade—
the deck of cards that would
no longer yield the queen
of diamonds on demand.
They were forced to find
another line of work,
since their shrinking
audience had given up
on the unexpected,
demanding facts and
nothing but.
People were tired
of enchantment.
The magicians loaded
their belongings into trunks
that would never
again house women
about to be halved, saving

the shiny metal tubes
for potting plants and
the white gloves for parties.
People sitting on screened
porches one summer afternoon
saw a trail of black capes
moving down Main Street
past the funeral homes.

Someone may still find
a broken hoop,
a paper flower petal,
or a silver-tipped wand
bent and left behind.

What Jazz Can Do

On an outdoor stage
four men play together;
and then stop to listen
to each man's solo
with the attention of a heart surgeon
or mother with her young child.
Two are Black. Two are white.
They play their instruments almost
faster than I can hear.
They all want to hit that blue note
just right and have us join in.

They show respect to each other
and the audience.
Sometimes they sing.
Sometimes they scat.
They bow heads toward the other
instead of applause.
Sometimes they joke.
Sometimes they laugh.
"Nobody loves me save my mama
and she may be jiving, too."

No allusion on that stage
to white cops yanking
Black women out of their cars
because they can.
No young Black boy gets shot
for pulling up his hoodie in the rain
while a shiftless white ne'er-do-well
sights him in his cross hairs.

On this stage and in our seats
everyone can breathe.
When they close their set
with, "When the Saints Go Marchin' In,"
and women, parasols overhead, dance in the aisles
the New Orleans-style second line,
we can believe at least tonight
that moment will come real soon.

Zelda

If she knew he'd lift
excerpts from her diaries
and write them into his stories
would she still have married him?

Pretending to take it lightly
she wrote in a review
that the famous author
believed "plagiarism begins at home."

She fell for him the night they met
but it wouldn't be
all splashing in fountains, sitting atop taxis,
and striking poses.

They'd drink till dawn, but for him
there was never enough booze. She wanted
to be a writer or dancer.
When she wrote an article on her own
his byline still came first.

She'd threaten to divorce him
but never follow through.
Where would she go?
What a fool not to learn a saleable skill.

He's famous for saying,
"There are no second acts in American life."

Though starting late in ballet, but training hard
Zelda received an offer from the San Carlo Opera,
Scott wouldn't let her accept,
he thought a rest cure more in order.

Yes, he was handsome, but so was her hairdresser.
Scott preferred her in a sanatorium in Switzerland.
Out of the way he would finish his novel.
Though that took quite a while.

Diagnosed with schizophrenia
by Dr. Bleuler, a colleague of Jung's,
who thought dance was bad for Zelda
as was anything else.
Bleuler found her a sad case.

She died not knowing she'd become
Scott's equal in renown.
How quickly a life can turn—
like milk left on the shelf
past its expiration date, suddenly reeking.

She died closer to home
in an Asheville hospital burned to the ground.
Scott thought himself the doting husband
though he'd filed her letters unread under Z.

Louis

The grandson of a slave
he landed in the Colored Waif's Home
at the age of eleven
for doing like others
and shooting a gun into the air on New Year's Eve.
Before that he rode with the Karnoffksys
on their junk wagon
helping to collect trash to resell.
That immigrant family helped
buy his first horn from a pawn shop.

As child prisoner
he learned to play so well
he became the leader of the Waif's Home Band.
They performed all over New Orleans.
When word got out
that he would march through his old haunts,
his neighbors, prostitutes and pimps,
his mother among them,
lined the street to watch and cheer.
He asked his teacher if he could pass the hat

and collected enough cash
to buy everyone new uniforms and instruments.
He never tried to hide his past.
The biggest lie he ever told was
about his birthday.
He wasn't born on the fourth of July:
Consider the pride of a black man
making that claim.

He played the cornet like no one else
and still his career moved in fits and starts.
Inept managers tied to the mob regularly
skimmed his paychecks.
The Great Depression forced band mates
into work as tailor or taxi driver,
another grew chickens.

Louis moved on to California,
insisting he live by the music he helped invent.
One may doubt his claim that
his whole life was happiness
but he never faked his smile
whether playing for audiences Black or white.
He signed his many letters:
Red beans and ricely yours, Louis.

Moonshine

Tell them I was beautiful
or maybe that's just moonshine.
Think of Icarus' wings
not as melting wax
but bits of broken glass
that in the sun's glare
blazed like gems.
Think of moonshine
not as bad booze
but false light.
And whether on delusion
or imagination
for a time that boy soared.

Angels

In the celestial hierarchy there are nine rungs:
Angels, archangels, principalities, powers, virtues,
dominions, thrones, cherubim, and seraphim.

The Pope says they're often misunderstood,
always invisible, still surely hovering
outside each precinct of the world.

I like to think of them sitting
in some abandoned union hall,
their wings tucked under carefully

as choir robes, as they patiently await
their assignments—whose life they'll
be obliged to bail out over and over

until its end.
Languishing in the sky between emergencies,
the angels blanket themselves in clouds,

cup their ears, and make way
for passing airplanes.
The need to believe in them keeps us conjuring

likenesses out of cotton and crepe paper,
glitter, glass, and cookie dough. For they are
the guardians of the second chance, the one

that gives you the heart to start over
in the middle of a life that has come to nothing.
They recall what you love when you're about to give up:

Words that resemble musical tones—alabaster,
cloisonné, periwinkle. The bells of the clock tower
chiming the quarter hour, as if to say

small steps will get you there,
the muffled sound of footfall on snow.
The white of ivory and pearls with which we endow them

springs from the spectrum, its promise that possibilities
persist, as each road seems to lead to a wall we can't scale
without the help of wings.

Part II

Eve's Version

He's off chatting with God
but when God's too busy
doing God knows what
then Adam tells me how lonely he was
before I came on the scene.
Between tilling the fields
and talking to the Big Guy
how he could get lonely beats me.
Everything whispers
and bubbles and shines.
Gorgeous trees, plants, and the lapping
of four rivers round our shores.
When I point out the loneliness
bespeaks a lack of inner resources
all of a sudden he's got something better to do.
So much for sweet talk.
If I should be a helper to him
then I should let him know
where there's room for improvement.
Like that tree in the middle of things
we're supposed to steer clear of.
God forbid we should know good from evil.
Evil must be elsewhere.
Meanwhile Adam's the only guy around.
Too bad he doesn't have more of an imagination.
And the flowers sure smell better.
Not to mention, it's the birds that can fly.
I'm supposed to listen to someone who
doesn't talk directly to me?
What's with that?
Forbidden fruit. C'mon.
Try this.

Anne Frank

"Everyone real or invented deserves the open destiny of life."
—Grace Paley

Anne Frank was born in 1929,
the same year as my mother.
I imagine a girl
penned in all day
in stocking feet, reading
an entire Dickens novel
and speaking to no one,
living on mealy potatoes
and hope, little flags pegged
on a map to mark the progress
of a liberating army that comes
just months too late.
Anne's just beginning to menstruate
and wonder about love.

*

An ocean away my mother,
the elder daughter of two Polish Jews
who paid an exit tax to leave their home,
sleeps on the living room couch
in their cold-water flat on Grand Street,
works in a hat factory on Sundays
for pocket money so that at age twelve
she can choose her own purple coat—
the color of queens, she later confides.

To hear her tell it, her father is fast becoming
a selfish bum, after all he's a failure,
schnorring pennies for the shul, instead of getting rich,
but I know her to be a liar.

Her first week in kindergarten it poured every day—
God's punishment for not telling
the clerk her real age.
She's a girl alone who trusts
money and weather maps
to deliver her. Rage spatters over
mother and father as she plots
her marriage at her desk in school.
It is her parents' own fault they are poor.

*

When movement's confined
to a few small rooms and the sky
is only glimpsed through
narrow windows, help seems
as far away as the stars.
Still, Anne covers the walls
around her cot with Hollywood studio pix
and reflects on what's become
of her friends.

I like to think of her as an adult
granted enough years to consider
forgiveness, to ponder
the uses of hatred.
We'd be out in the open, perhaps a park
where the sun is so strong
we must shade our eyes.
We're talking about groceries or hemlines
or a book just read.
We don't wear yellow stars
sewn on our sleeves.
I could be her daughter.

Emily

A man who's published many books
of verse told me Dickinson never
learned the rules of punctuation,
so she cheated with dashes. No way.

She bound her pages by hand.
Stitching them together
meant more to her
than canning fruit or making jam.

Till this day some people say she was quaint
or crazy. Aren't all poets—worrying
too much about line breaks, too little
about money? Staying home, baking pies,

making poems. To other people they're variations on a theme.
She sewed the pages of her little books
and hid them in her room for someone else to find.
She wanted hope to prevail over each day's prose—

possibilities distilled into words like no one else's.
What matters is she just wrote and wrote and wrote.

Pearl

She was only at ease onstage,
shouting when she sang herself hoarse.
A reporter asked
if she'd attended her prom.
She admitted, "No one asked me."

"Who needs women for friends when there are guys?"
Making love with everyone in sight
didn't make them love her.
Men ruled here and females earned fame
only as girlfriends. She still became a star,

but she never stopped hurting.
When press wolves surrounded her
she wrapped a feather boa round her precious throat;
dove to the bottom of bottles of Wild Turkey
and drug vials just to keep on.

Did she really know
Freedom's just another word
for nothing left to lose?
She was dead at twenty-seven.
You tell me.

You Think You Got Problems?

My brother tended to his flock
and I to my garden.
Abel praised God with the best of his herd
while I wasn't so fussy
and offered the first greens
I could lay my hands on.
A gesture, you know.
Isn't it supposed to be the thought that counts?
Well apparently not.
The Lord thanked Abel for what he gave
but not me.
And when that ticked me off
God whistled his breath
right down my back and warned, "Watch out—
sin's right at your door with his welcome mat."

I had other ideas and invited my showoff brother
for a walk in my field.
Then I picked up a rock from the friendly ground
and *zetzed* him a good one
right across that prissy *panim* of his.
He fell and the color faded from his face.
"Abel, enough, get up. I'm not angry anymore."
But my brother didn't hear me.
He would not answer. I finally got it.
He was as dead to the world
as the animals he sacrificed.
No one told me
bones break when struck—
that there are things you can't undo.
And all that blood.
What will I tell our mother?

Isaac's Sacrifice

His father's eyes were his mirror.

They woke early that morning.
With Mother still sleeping
they slipped away.

Isaac followed
the path his father chose
to the land of Moriah.

Only there
three days later did he ask
where they'd find the animal
for slaughter.

Then Isaac climbed the mountain,
carried the wood,
and placed his head on the sacred altar.

Just before the ax fell
he looked up for his father's face,
But the sun flared behind him
like a crown of anger
and Isaac closed his eyes.

His father was old and tired.
And what had he ever asked of his son?

Imelda

A woman intent
on a Webster's entry
understands the meaning of success.

"I am opulence,"
she boasts on the evening news.
"Imeldific will be in the dictionary."

They'll print her legacy
right after *imbrute*
and *imbue* on page 601.

The woman who wore a ball gown to her arraignment
has one hell of a sense of history:
She wants to be a word.

Union Square

About to board the train
a father busied himself talking with his older girl.
Left on her own the younger daughter,
instead of planting both feet firmly, slipped
through the slim crack between car and platform.
Only the reflex to throw out her arms saved her
as she crashed down on her elbows.
From the waist up she was visible
while her legs dangled dangerously near the rails.
A stranger lifted her to safety before she could cry.
How small the space between breathing and not.
And then the trained pulled out of the station on its way.

Brooklyn Bound

As if posed for a picture called "Restless Youth"

three kids stand on the footbridge
that spans the Stillwell Avenue station
and look out past the trains and concession

Stands of Coney Island—Nathan's Famous, a palace built
for the hot dog, and Disco Beat Bumper Cars—
toward the ocean and the subtler blue of the sky.

Did they catch the Mermaid Parade
that afternoon on the Boardwalk?
Women and girls in glitter and green blankets

enthroned in wagons and wheel chairs,
flapped their fin-bound legs
when reminded by their mothers

welcoming summer to Brooklyn shores.
As the mermaids rolled by, the Aqua String Band played along
pulling everyone's attention off the water, the horizon

and its promise of no limits.
It's Saturday, only 4 o'clock—what else have they to do?
Hours of daylight before them, the kids

hesitate before boarding the train
that bends achingly, as beautiful in the arc of its tracks
as the flight of any bird away from the water.

Too Hip for Its Own Good

People come here by the thousands now.
Some of them never get off the tourist bus.
What are they looking for?

Is it the sight of the famous bridge they walked across the other
    day?
The view of the skyline seen across the river,
its spires aspiring toward the sky while
still planted on the ground? Though it happens that some fall
    down.

I bet they missed the Bible I spotted
the other day left out in a downpour on a park bench
near the courthouse. Its leaves were bent
back like some rain forest flower.

Hope lives here as it does in many neighborhoods.
Still not everyone journeying to this oh-so-cool burgh can boast
that when they arrived their prayers were answered.

Afterward

Sometimes at palace balls
lights leap off the marble floors,
but before each dance there's a fitting
and standing still for hours.
"Always smile."
That's what the prince keeps telling me.
He walks the halls muttering to himself.

Each day is stretched on its long frame.
I stay in bed till noon,
then the afternoon stands still.

I search the water
in the garden pond,
but there's only the bottom,
and the coins I threw in for luck
the first night I came here.

Maybe I should study French.
I've learned the names of all the flowers
around the palace.
Next week I try the constellations.

I keep up on the new dance steps,
practicing with the chef's third assistant
who prefers to let me lead.

I think Charming's taken a lover.
I think he thinks he made a mistake.
I looked best in moonlight.

Maybe it will be better
when I become queen
or learn to play the cello.
I've seen pumpkins
turned into carriages.
Maybe it's all downhill from there.

Rosie

That's the secret, Nick. Smile. Even if I'm
singing a sad song I smile. People like to
believe everything will turn out all right.
— Rosemary Clooney, 1928–2002

In a small Kentucky town
a girl and her sister live with their granny.
Her baby brother Nick's off in California
with their mother who loves to sell things
more than she loves the role of mom.
She promised when she left
she'd be back for them real soon.
She never comes.

Dad drinks. He's around town, but no good.
Rosie knows this 'cause Mom said so.
But he comes around sometime
for dinner and it's a treat.
And when they've cleared the table
Dad and Rosie and her sister Betty all sing.
Hymns and pop songs tumble onto the table.
Dad tells her she sounds just fine.
He doesn't need to; Rosie knows.

Some winters in Maysville there's no money for fuel.
But Granny's got grit.
She cooks meals on a fire grate.
People gotta eat.
Everybody. Not just family.
Rosie and Betty bring friends
to supper. There's always some more
at the bottom of the pot.

While she's still in high school
Rosie and Betty sing on the radio—
sing in a band. And while still a kid,
she comes to New York.
She meets all kinds of characters.
Mitch Miller. Jose Ferrer.
And she cuts records.
So that we can be reminded

that "Autumn in New York—
it's good to live it again."
That wherever she travels
she's still got, "sweet Kentucky ham
on her mind." And whatever happens
"still it's a real good bet
the best is yet to come."
Please raise a glass to Rosie

who was dealt a crap hand
but didn't seem to know;
who married the wrong man first;
got lost in show biz glitz, pills,
and booze; fell apart but even did that
kind of funny.
As she ran streaking out of a hospital ward
someone in surgical scrubs asked,

"Who the hell is that?"
And Rosie shouted back
over her shoulder,
"Well it sure ain't Patti Page."

Damn straight!

Arshile Gorky

He hadn't done anything wrong
and yet his past was the secret he never told.
He made up a story
that became his life before painting.
Made up his name too.
Didn't admit he was Armenian.
Depending on his mood
he was either Russian or Georgian
and Josef Stalin could do no wrong.
At birth he was Vostaneg Adoian
from the village of Van,
son of Sedrak and Shusan.
Claimed he was Maxim Gorky's nephew,
not knowing the writer too
had changed his name.
Told people his father was dead
when he'd only moved to Watertown.
When the man finally died
Gorky couldn't publicly mourn.
His mother died years before
when a hospital back home denied her a bed.
He didn't go to school,
but claimed he graduated
from Brown, an engineering major, no less.
While dating a woman
whose father was an athlete
to seem more of a guy's guy
he bragged he was Brown's
long-jump champion.
After all he was tall.

Why not? He was as talented
a liar as a painter.
People took him at his word.
Get him talking, he'd go on all night,
but some things never came up.
No one knew that as a child
he'd seen the corpses of neighbors
piled high in the town square.
He survived cancer
but chose to hang himself
a few years later in a barn.

Even his wife didn't know
the stories he told about himself
were just another work of art.

Art, Credo

Someone…will have to attend, for a time only, the great university of poverty…

—Vincent van Gogh

He drew the sower and the reaper,
the man dragging a harrow across his field.
The sorrow he mapped in the faces of peasants and workers
became his religion. They mattered more to him
than owners of mansions or the kingdom of heaven.

His storm clouds fill with the voice of God.
The paintings were his prayer book.

Even when he turned his brush into a fire hose
that spewed his oils in fevered tiers
of irises like pennants, cypress and olive trees
twisting beseechingly toward the sky,

blossoming almonds delicate as butterflies
Vincent was not satisfied or soothed;
maybe by all those wheat fields
or blooming orchards under cornflower skies,
his narrow bedroom with its childish red blanket,
the only room where he ever slept through the night,

the straw chair on which he set his beloved pipe,
or the interior garden of the madhouse
where he hoped he'd find peace of mind.

Even after he weathered storms of breakdowns
without irony he'd quote Dr. Pangloss,
"Everything is always for the best in the best of worlds."

In his shambled mind Vincent never grasped
that his paintings were beautiful.

Though Theo was younger, a few months later he followed
his brother to the grave. His wife Johanna soon
had him exhumed so Theo and Vincent
could lie side by side in the Auvers-sur-Oise cemetery
for what passes for eternity in this faithless world.

Chuck Jones Tribute

Let's hear it for the talking rabbit
who keeps a shaggy monster
from devouring him
by offering a manicure.
"Monsters must lead such *in-t-e-r-e-s-t-i-n-g* lives!"
he purrs with aplomb as he files his claws.
Let's hear it for the bunny
who befuddles his hunter
insisting it's duck not rabbit season,
so he's off limits.
Let's hear it for our hero
as he outsmarts a hound
three times his size by luring him
into a hollowed-out log
that leads right off a cliff.

And let's hear it for the man who dreamt them up.

Hurrah for the desert-dwelling coyote,
Acme Merchandise's best customer,
forever chasing a bird with a do
a rock star would wear proudly.
He can outrun a race car
whatever the obstacle lying in his path.
The upright piano launched from above
or the tautly tied pyramid of TNT are no match for him.
"Beep beep!" he mocks and moves on.

But *suffering succotash!* Who's this?
It's our former fearless leader, George the W.
and he was stalking the real deal,
the genuine evil-doers—
no talking animals for him.

And he'd warned *new-kew-ler* strike,
a weapon he could wield but never pronounce.

So let's give thanks to Chuck Jones who animated
a sputtering duck with a sibilant *s* and a big vocabulary,
a rabbit who truly knows what's up and his dimwitted pursuer,
all far easier to take than life as we know it.

No Man Quite Like Him

Bob Moses chose to go south.
He was from Harlem,
not Mississippi.
He left Harvard

to encourage Black people to try to vote.
In the sixties that
was a crazy risk in Mississippi.

Only uppity niggers dared climb
the courthouse stairs to sign up
with a registrar who often couldn't read,
but would still ask them

to explain some obscure clause
in the constitution of Mississippi.
On the way down a deputy

would be waiting to arrest them
after taking a few swipes with his billy club
for their disturbance of the peace of Mississippi
and cart them off to jail.

For the sheriff and his staff
the law was an inside joke
Negroes would never get in Mississippi.
An ass-whupping was another matter.

Moses went to jail too
where he caught up on his Camus in Mississippi.
Still he convinced others to join him

walk to the courthouse again and again
in the hot sun of Mississippi.
Moses dressed like a farmer wearing
overalls and a T-shirt

and preferred hearing what others
had to say before he spoke.
Gently, he moved people toward change

one step at a time
back when there was no place in America
quite like Mississippi.

Heavens, No

If there's no heaven or heaven on earth
what's all this suffering for?
A Black man opens his front door
and is greeted by a policeman's gun.

All this suffering because
a man can be killed without breaking the law,
greeted by a policeman's gun
while reaching for his identification.

If a man can be killed without breaking the law
why must he try to live by the rules?
It's a reach to expect him to identify or comply
with those who wish he were still in chains.

Unfairly he's forced to live by the rules
though there's no heaven on earth
and too many people want him in chains.
A Black man can't just open his door and move on.

If there's no heaven
what's all this suffering for?

Susan B.

rode west by train or wagon
to outposts she'd never seen before.
Stepped down from the coach
onto craggy streets huddled over
by shanties and saloons
and asked where there was a hall
large enough to hold a crowd.
That's how she'd announce she had come to town.

After she spoke she slept on cots
or straw in stoveless rooms in rundown inns.
Woke up the next day and broke
the ice frozen overnight
on the rim of a tin basin so she could wash.
That ice was the mirror in which
she saw her face for years.
She rode alone, refusing failure
then died more than a decade
before women won the right to vote.

Alice Paul

Because other suffragists
were too tame
she broke away
and started the National Women's Party.
Her bedroom was in its headquarters:
her only life and home.
Her only friends
were sister militants.
She'd push herself again and again
until collapse and hospital stays.

She lost her sense of smell after
too many tubes thrust up her nose
as they forced-fed in her prison.
Men hardly stood by pleasantly
when she marched for the cause.
She and her cohort
were spat upon and smacked,
beaten to the ground;
as if her foes didn't see
Paul weighed barely ninety pounds.

She stenciled Woodrow Wilson's
own words about freedom onto a banner
and went to jail for that, too.
As soon as women won the right to vote
She drafted the first text
of the Equal Rights Amendment.
She lived long enough to see
Congress vote to approve
and died believing
it would soon be law.

How She Came Here

In Slovakia when she was eight
her dad said it would be fun
to take a vacation. Before the start of school.

she, her sister, Mom and Dad
went to a port town across the sea.
Cramped for months into a single room

they crammed English
by watching all TV shows not dubbed
into Italian. She asked when vacation

would end, worried always about being late.
Dad would answer, "Look how much you're learning.
Isn't this fun and just like school?"

A year later they landed here,
started Anna in South Slope's
P.S. 70, while she kept asking

when they could go home.
Soon. Not yet. Soon.
As an adult she finally found out why.

Back then Dad had been named
"a person of interest"
to the state. Had they stayed put

and not started their long vacation
he'd have been arrested, jailed
the rest of them expelled,

languishing while awaiting
his release, which might not ever come—
this launched her into a new land

and language without fair warning,
rehearsed for in a low-budget hotel—
an unintentional immigrant

always looking over her shoulder toward home.

Fabulous Joe

Say you've been arrested and interned
as a young man in wartime just because
you're a foreigner. From then on
you want to go anywhere you wish
with the ease of a single breath. So as you
start out on your great adventure
to New York when it's still the beacon
to the best in every field
you start to change your story.

You omit leaving
your small German town,
cutting all ties to your parents
over a quarrel you never admit;
don't mention the first wife you desert.

Take it from there.
It's your damn story and who's
going to contradict you?
So when you set up your business
in a building full of boxing gyms
where the likelihood
of sharing space with two
iconic dance studios

is slim to nil, who cares?
Who will find out?
Of course, you don't know
that George Balanchine
is still in Paris, so it's impossible
you two met as you claimed.
He was dancing in a small troupe
across the ocean, not down the hall.

When you were still in Europe you boast
you were you a boxer, a circus acrobat,
a model for medical illustrators,
a self-defense trainer
for a major police force;
or none of the above?
We'll never know for sure.
In New York you crave
to become not just famous,
but a nonpareil.
You created an exercise system
that you knew would change
the way people stood and slept and breathed.

The better your story
the more people take note.
Your lies were charming
and hurt no one.
You did your best P.T. Barnum
on your own behalf.
Hokum and bluster sell tickets.
Your favorite fairy tale was your fabulous biography.

Forty years later your schemes worked.
People practice what you taught
by the millions worldwide.
People were so impressed
with your workouts
your disciples fought in court
just to own rights to them. The problem is
you didn't live to see any of it—

but in the end, you got just what you wanted.

Lee Miller

She fled Poughkeepsie for Paris
and went from Man Ray's model
to an artist in her own right,
photographing the ordinary
and the bizarre, but always
from an odd angle.
But after the war
and the photos of Dachau
she never recovered.
Admitting she was in over
her head, she put her camera away,
hid in the kitchen, devising
strange recipes while downing martinis.
She won dozens of contests
creating advertising slogans
and abandoned thousands of negatives
in the attic, found by her son after she died.
She'd been raped at seven
and photographed nude
by her burgher father.
A woman can reinvent herself just so many times.

Dorothea's Foot

She came from money,
not what you'd expect
for the photographer of "Migrant Mother,"
icon of the Dust Bowl.
Not buckets but enough to be middle class.
She first set up shop
taking society portraits
of well-heeled San Franciscans.
Then brought those skills with her
when she wandered among
shanty-cluttered transient camps
where the jobless huddled
in lean-tos like rats' nests.
They'd lost their homes,
but not the need to feed their young.
Lange talked with each person
before she snapped the picture,
sometimes climbing atop her truck for the best shot.
The only self-portrait she ever took
was for a class she taught late in life
called "Where I Live."
It's an image of her polio-warped foot,
that walked her closer
to people regarded by others
who hadn't lost everything
as so much lazy trash.

Languishing in Plain Sight

My country pretends to shine,
but in my neighborhood
beggars linger on every corner.
Who cares if the sad song they
isn't their real story?
Who would sit on a cardboard box all day
if he had somewhere better to be?

Neighbors leave empty bottles
near their for doors for street dwellers
to redeem for change
that might buy a meal or a fix.

Last week a man asked me for food
and I offered him one of the three
baskets of berries I'd just bought.
"What else you got?" he asked.
He gave the berries back saying,
"Don't worry, honey, my hands are clean."

Since we've started
calling our country the homeland
it's less welcoming than ever.
It's not what I remember being taught at school
or tucked in my bed thinking I was safe.

Burning

A five-year-old hiding from the Nazis
in a Christian orphanage catches an adult
whisper about the red haze smudging
a window, "The Jews are burning."

A Palestinian farmer wakes at night
from anxious sleep. The well is far
behind the house. How can it help while
his grandfather's olive grove is burning?

American pilots drop chemicals
quickly to clear obscuring foliage.
Napalm also sticks to skin and all America
watches a girl running down the road burning.

During the civil war in Syria
a despot bombs his own people.
One hundred thousand are already dead,
an ancient Aleppo minaret is burning.

In the American South Black people
fighting for the right to vote take
truncheon blows to the head or bullets in spines
while their homes and churches keep burning.

These fires flare up through history.
The scars they leave
don't heal. Still man's hunger for war
keeps burning.

How Did this Happen?

The prophet Isaiah demanded his people
be a light unto the world.
He was a scold.
By his word the Jews
never quite measured up.
He unleashed his screed
more than two thousand years ago
but the Old Testament notion
that trouble and sorrow
visit people who stray
stuck with me.

Didn't the current citizens of Israel
go to Hebrew school, too?
How can they stop ambulances
at checkpoints
keeping their Palestinian neighbors
from emergency rooms?
Why do soldiers fire
high-powered rifles at children
even if they're throwing rocks?
Who marks apartheid roads—
one for Jews and one for Arabs?
How can people without a home for millennia
steal anyone else's land?
What happened to the light
we were supposed to be?
Where did it go?

Curious George

Curiouser and curiouser…

The elusive little monkey
whose miniature clay likeness
I sought for years to add to my collection
wielded far more power than I knew—

In the books I loved from childhood
George didn't just upend the proverbial apple cart,
he was always protected by
his unflappable keeper,
the man in the yellow hat.
George always messed up and triumphed.

Decades before these minor missteps
he rescued people with less guile
than the run-of-the-mill superhero
or local detective.

--

The urge to make trouble,
that lives buried in timid little girls like me
with good grades and pleasing faces,
almost fills the curio cabinets inside their hearts
like so many lace hankies
with stains so small you might not notice.
Only later the shelves get cluttered
with the less dainty *shmattas*
of miscues and disappointments.

--

When the Reys, the imp's creators tried to cross
a seemingly impermeable border,

the Nazi guard who asked to see their papers
found sketches of a small monkey cartwheeling
across a neighborhood of bristol board.

Tired and impatient, perhaps bored with his job,
the brown-shirted functionary
was charmed by the monkey,
then known as Fifi.

And even though they were Jews
he chuckled and waved them through.

That Statue

standing in the harbor
with the poem carved into its base
bears an invitation
to the luckless to come right in.
She's family, a *landsman*
because the woman
who wrote the verse was a Jew
whose family also traveled far from elsewhere.
These days hatred and suspicion

of any stranger is applauded, popular.
When in doubt call the cops.
Our country is the homeland now
and we get to say who can visit,
who can stay; what small child
or young mother we can return to
country of origin as if the process
is not painless. And we were only pushing
pencils, papers, not people.

Meanwhile in plain sight
that statue though growing older
has turned green, not with envy,
but the color of a fresh spring
when starting over is the order of the day.
That statue still wants to light the way in.
But she can't talk, so it's easy not to listen.

Poem Without a Solution

Half way round the world
there's so little I can do
for the small Syrian child
covered in blood-soaked clothes.

Still in the news photo
he looks up and juts out his chin
as he says to the soldiers surrounding him,
"I'm going to tell God on you."

Leap of Faith

Whether I light Sabbath candles
on time or not at all
is only my affair.
So when the eager young woman
comes between my friend and me
on the street to ask
Excuse me are you Jewish?
I always lie.

What I love and whom I believe
is strictly up to me.
My prayers are only mine and always private.
But my father who died years ago
took his faith with him across the ocean.
Running from the Nazis kept him motivated
the rest of his short life.
On his *yahrzeit* I light a candle
that blazes while I sleep.

Disappeared

the Kentile Floor sign its neon seen
from the lurching F train

the dome of One Hanson Place
visible from any direction

before glass cubes blocked the view
the Gotham Book Mart

my local library that we fought
so hard to save

space to walk on the Brooklyn Bridge
the tiny shop on Seventh Avenue

that sold handmade jewelry
Fassbinder's in the Village

Aunt Helen's Restaurant
fresh mozzarella from Aiello's Latticeria on Court Street

Café Edison in the theater district
where I ate with Arto before a show

he's gone, too, ten years
affordable Broadway tickets

the Brooklyn Works billboard by the piers
a city catering to its citizens not its tourists

my health
the Kentile Floors sign

the Kentile Floors sign
the Kentile Floors sign

About the Author

Barbara Elovic has published poems in more than one hundred journals, which include *Poetry, Sonora Review,* and *Marlboro Review*. Additionally, her work is included in anthologies
published by Scribners, Dell, and Columbia University Press. Bright Hill Press published her chapbook, *Other People's Stories,* in late 2014. Her first chapbook, *Time Out,* appeared in 1996. She's been nominated for a Pushcart Prize. She served as one of the founding editors of the New York-based poetry journal, *Heliotrope*. In midlife she left her career in trade books behind to become a Pilates instructor. She lives in Brooklyn.

www.ingramcontent.com/pod-product-compliance
Lightning Source LLC
Chambersburg PA
CBHW020313090426
42735CB00009B/1320